BIG Gemini Kennels

DEDICATION

"This book is dedicated to the two XL American Bully Legends I was blessed enough to own. To the one that I created, BGK's Cujo, and the one which I raised, BGK's Rock. You were the best friend I ever had." - Andre Smith

www.BigGeminiKennels.com

|TABLE OF CONTENTS

XL American Bully Legends: The Evolution

Hello again dog lovers worldwide, it is I, Andre Smith of Big Gemini Kennels. You may know me as the XL American Bully breeder extraordinaire, and more importantly for this list, a well-versed dog historian. I have been both in love and involved with the American Bully breed for about 15-16 years. Currently, I have eighteen XL American Bullies on my properties, all of which I love dearly. I don't know if they are a part of my family or if I am a part of their pack at this point, ha! Regardless, what I do know is that I love and respect this breed, (and my dogs), more than I trust most human beings.

The American Bully is a very special and versatile breed capable of playing a wide variety of roles. With their families, they are the ultimate loving, affectionate, clingy companion, who want nothing more than ever to please and protect their loved ones. However, with strangers, they are the face of terror when encountering a threat; they are willing to shred them to pieces and fight to the death to protect their family. They possess an imposing physique, dense muscle structure, and intimidating looks that would make anyone second-guess entering their property. They have a strong drive, a high intelligence level, and are very strong-willed. With that being said, these dogs require a dominant personality to keep them in their place and maintain the proper hierarchical structure that a pack needs to function efficiently.

I have seen American Bullies do great personal protection work, performing stellar acts such as: being a hunting dog, service dog work, working alongside law enforcement officers, search and rescue work, weight pulling, etc. I have yet to see a task that this special breed is unable to perform. I decided to write this book to accompany my

Youtube video documenting the rise of XL American Bully legends which have molded and shaped the XL American Bully breed into what it is today. Here is the link to my Youtube video: https://youtu.be/zwUym7uewcl. I think it is very important that a credible source documents these canine legends which have had such an incredible influence on the American Bully community so that their stories and legends can be told to those looking to research the breed in the future. With that being said, I have decided to take it upon myself to curate this list. I feel that it is a matter of utmost importance to permanently preserve this portion of American Bully History. For full disclosure, I am blessed to have owned two of the dogs on the XL American Bully legend list. They have only been included as a part of this list because the American Bully community as a whole agrees that they have earned the right to be listed, not because of a personal bias.

The American Bully breed is not nearly as well known or recognized as it should be at this stage of its development. They do not get credit or publicity; in fact, it's long overdue. The breed as a whole is often overlooked, so much so that people tend to confuse American Bullies for Pitbulls and the other way around. I care deeply for this breed and believe that it deserves a clear definition of not only the breed as a whole but more importantly, legendary foundation dogs that the XL

American Bully world is built upon.

To this day, I haven't seen anyone give these amazing dogs the recognition they truly deserve. I am yet to see anyone thoroughly document the American Bully breed and their legends/foundation dogs, as well as the lasting impact which they have had on this emerging breed. For people to gain a true understanding of The American Bully, they will need to understand the breed's history, as well as be familiar with the founding influential dogs which contributed to the foundation of the Bully movement. They need to understand which legendary dogs helped to build this breed so that they can see how the breed has evolved into the different forms and styles that we see today.

There are multiple types of American Bullies. More specifically, the American Bully Kennel Club (commonly referred to as ABKC) categorized the Bully breed into the following five classes: (1) Pocket, (2) Classic, (3) Standard, (4) Extreme, and (5) XL. Micro-American Bullies could also be included depending on who you speak to. However, since I am an experienced XL American Bully breeder myself, we are going to focus on the XL class, and the legends within that class, (with some honorable mentions as well).

The reason I will be separating legends and honorable

mentions is because I view them as two separate categories. When I reference XL legends, I tend to think about dogs that have been well known in the Bully community and made a huge impact within the breed itself. Also, to be considered a legend, the dog must have had legendary offspring, of equal caliber to itself or better; carrying unprecedented production power despite the gender of the dog. Legends also have to have legendary production power and consistently produce dogs of their caliber or better, regardless of the female they are bred to. This is vital so that their offspring can continue on their "legacy". This is the only way that they can effectively have a lasting impact on the breed. In addition, legends helped to determine what style of dog different breeders preferred and helped them to discover what style of XL American Bullies they'd like to produce, myself included. I believe this impact is *extremely* important, hence the difference between the two categories; the strength and longevity of the impacts that legendary dogs made not only in the dog community but on the general public as well. True legends transcended simply by being popular in the American Bully world and helped to introduce the general public to the new breed. According to Webster's Dictionary, the technical definition of "legend", is as follows: An important or famous person known for doing something extremely well. In this case, we can substitute the word "*person*" for "*dog*" for a better fit.

Legendary American Bullies are notably known for their unique ability to produce. This is important when we determine who is a legend because if these dogs cannot consistently produce offspring of like quality to themselves, they cannot contribute to the breed, and therefore have no lasting impact. There are also a few more exhaustive definitions available for the term legend that would best fit our image. The term "legend" also has a fuller definition and describes it as a thing or person which inspires, in this case, that would be an XL American Bully (https://www.merriam-webster.com/dictionary/legend). I believe that this definition of a legend is the best fit for the legends we are discussing because if you have a dog that has a desirable temperament, outstanding character traits, and high reproduction value, then it can be defined as "a dog that can inspire". Another standard I believe that the legends on the list should be held to is: Do they produce producers? If a legend is truly a "super producer" it will lead to more impressive productions from his offspring, which will inevitably have a long-lasting impact on the bloodline as a whole. When it comes to honorable mentions, I want to clarify that just because they happen to fall under a separate category from legends, it does not necessarily mean that they are not important. A dog can only be an honorable mention if it played a significant role in establishing or influencing the XL American Bully breed. The honorable mentions are either on their way to becoming legends, or they died prematurely and, sadly, did not complete enough productions to become a legend. If you understand dogs, then you will comprehend why I either did or did not include certain dogs in this list.

Before we discuss who the legends are in the XL American Bully community, I would like to first establish some facts about the breed. The Pitbull breed as a whole dates back to the early 1800s, originally founded in the United Kingdom. The American Bully breed is a newer companion breed first established and recognized by the American Bully Kennel Club (ABKC) in 2004. The breed was then recognized by the European Bully Kennel Club in 2008. The third recognition came from what I believe to be the most prestigious of all three registries to recognize the American Bully Breed, the United Kennel Club (UKC), in 2013. So, as you can see, this breed is still evolving and fairly new.

An XL American Bully is defined as large males standing at about 20-23 inches tall at the withers, and females at about 19-22 inches. On average, XL Bullies, weigh 80-150 pounds. The XL American Bully has an impressive athletic build, which is both muscular and defined, displaying great strength and agility. Typically, the breed shows physical traits such as large bulky heads, high chests, broad shoulders, thick rears, etc. Bullies are versatile and high-functioning, capable of accomplishing a wide variety of tasks. Overall, the XL Bully breed is full of dogs who are well-rounded, trustworthy, and would make ideal family companions. As a matter of fact, check out https://biggeminikennels.com if you're looking for the *perfect* companion for you and your family! In order for the Bully community to expand, we must reach the general public because they are the most important audience for one's own business. The American Bully community needs to effectively infiltrate mainstream media and spread accurate information to educate the masses. By doing so, the breed can become just as well known as any other breed, on a larger scale.

As we approach this list of XL American Bully legends, which I have curated, I want it to be made known that I am not covering this subject matter from a biased perspective, but rather as a dog enthusiast and historian documenting the founding legends which have had the greatest influence on the breed. This can be proven by my inclusion of certain kennels who have lost my respect. No matter how I feel about certain owners/ kennels, I know that their dogs have legitimately earned their place on this legendary list and in XL American Bully history; so credit must be given where it is due. My personal feelings are irrelevant when it comes to documenting historical facts about the American Bully breed.

Facts over feelings is one of my favorite mottos. That being said, I, Dre of Big Gemini Kennels, was **not biased** while creating this list. Considering that I have been dealing with this breed since roughly 2005, I have been there from the inception of the XL American Bully breed. I can tell you who started it and who was a part of building the foundation of the breed which I love and will forever be an ambassador for, The American Bully. Let's examine these American Bully Legends, as well as the Honorable mentions. *If you are a breeder or dog lover who wants to maximize the potential of your puppy or begin a successful top-quality breeding program, my other book is absolutely for you! Check it out!*

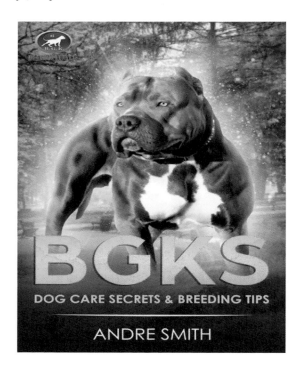

XL American Bully Legends

1. Juan Gotty of Gottiline

Pedigree: https://www.pitpedia.com/dog/notorious-juan-gotty/

Although this list is in no particular order, I believe that this dog deserves to go first. This will be the only one that is in a certain order. Moving forward, Juan Gotty was named after the notorious gangster Juan Gotty by Richard Barajas who purchased him. The dog was purchased for only $1,300 from the OG Tony Moore, (R.I.P.) of Greyline Kennels. That price was an unbelievable steal if you ask me. Juan Gotty is the son of Gray Line's Raider. Raider was bred to his daughter, PR Gray Lines Calle Love Bluegood, making Juan Gotty an inbred dog. However, this fact is not common knowledge to many. Gotti Pitbull Line, also known as Gotti Line, was founded by Richard Barajas, former owner of Westside Kennels who owned the legendary Juan Gotty. His bloodline became one of the most popular American Bully lines after it was established. If you did not know who Juan Gotty was, then I hate to tell you, but you are not fully knowledgeable of the Bully world at all. Juan Gotty has one of the most infamous pictures of all American Bullies to date (see above). As previously stated, Richard Barajas purchased Juan Gotty for only $1,300, and he bought it from Tony Moore. Can you believe that? It only took $1,300 to begin the foundation for the American Bully breed. Tony Moore, the owner and founder of Greyline Kennels, was based in Los Angeles, California. This means that Juan Gotty's blood goes back to Greyline Kennels. Which is not surprising if you understand the full impact of this dog. He just so happens to be the grandfather of BGK's The Rock, but not just him. There are a lot of famous dogs who share blood with Juan Gotty. This is why he should be regarded as an XL American Bully legend. He is one of the main founding fathers of the breed. It is said that Juan Gotty was 100% APBT. He is an important pillar in the Bully community and should continue to be valued as such. Although Juan Gotty is not technically an XL American Bully, he did lead to the development and creation of the class.

He sired over 900-1200 UKC registered offspring. If you own a Bully today, chances are Juan Gotty is somewhere in your pedigree if you look far back enough. Going back to the definition of a legend, when it comes to XL American Bullies, we must look at the impact. Not many had a more impressive and long-lasting influence on the bloodline than Juan Gotty. However, being a legend does not come without its faults. Several rumors were considered common knowledge among the Bully community about this dog. One of the rumors was that he was put on steroids. It has been alleged that most of his offspring came from his brother due to his inability to reproduce while being on steroids. Whether the rumor is true or not, that's up to you to decide. I have heard this rumor first-hand many times from credible respected breeders.

2. West-Side Monster aka Monster Jojola

Pedigree: https://www.pitpedia.com/dog/monster-jojola/

This legendary beast is pretty much one of the forefathers of the XL American Bully that created the highly sought-after Bully geno phenotype which is still popular to this day. He is a direct descendant of the legendary Juan Gotty and in his prime was one of the most sought-after American Bully studs. Westside Monster was composed of mostly OG Greyline blood and was owned and bred by Richard Barajas himself. Everyone wanted to breed this amazing specimen and many considered him to be the new and improved version of his father Juan Gotty. He proved his father to be a super-producer by consistently reproducing and outproducing himself, breeding after breeding. Many kennels such as Sunline, Blueline, Sharkline, etc. used this amazing stud to create incredible offspring that carried on Monster's impressive physical attributes as well as his legacy. Westside Monster's contributions to the newly formed XL American Bully breed are super impressive and simply undeniable. His look, his production power, and his temperament became highly sought after and everyone still loves this body style to this very day. To call him an American Bully Legend is an understatement. His influence on the breed still remains well over a decade later. Some of his more notable offspring include Monster's Rain, Leon's Goliath, Lomell's Da Hoodrat Blueline, Sunline's We Rollin' Solo, Pates Chantilly Lace, and so many more.

3. King Lion of Royal Blue Generation

Pedigree: https://www.pitpedia.com/dog/rbgs-king-lion/

King Lion is widely recognized as one of the first XL American Bully legends. This dog had a tremendous impact on the community and me as well. He was one of my favorite dogs to come from the American Bully world, and when I think of the first XL American Bullies, I recognize King Lion as the rightful earner of that coveted spot. He was owned by Saul Servantes, a good friend of mine, and a fellow *Gemini*. He collaborated with Tiffany of Able Paws to create the incredible legend we now know as King Lion. He was one of the first XL American Bully legends to go to a dog show and shut it down, leaving the people amazed by his size, structure, temperament, and overall look. He looked and acted like a super-sized Pitbull with much more size and girth. This dog had a lot of fire and drive, and people love to see that in XL American Bullies, myself included. He earned his name to the fullest. He was a beast like a lion that acted like a king; thus, the name King Lion. He earned his name to the fullest. There is a famous photo of King Lion facing off with Stone (one of the honorable mentions).

This photo accurately depicts a common practice at the earlier bully shows where the owners would face their dogs off, and not for the reason you might think. They did not do it because they wanted to see them fight. The real reason for the "faceoff" was to display the fire and drive which burned within them. Giving their Alpha Male a chance to shine in front of the dog show attendees. Even though most of these

dogs were not champions, they were deemed champions within the Bully community due to the tremendous impact that they had. King Lion's true trophies were his incredible productions.

He was a proven super-producer, and I love to see a dog that can throw a lot of offspring just as good as the original or better. He produced Disciple, King Liger, Jalisco, Ghostface (aka Blue Line's Smokey), etc. King Lion had a very impressive production history, he even produced a super-sized beautiful female that I owned, Queen Kali. The King's legacy is undeniable. When Roman of Iron-Cross Kennels decided to take Q-Ball and breed her back to King Lion, he made XL Bully history by creating ICK's Disciple, who went on to become a super-producer himself. The fact that King Lion could produce an impressive producer significantly adds to his legendary status. Shout out to Saul and RBG Kennels for creating this legend and helping to form the XL American Bully community!

4. Disciple of Iron-Cross Kennels

Pedigree: https://www.pitpedia.com/dog/iron-cross-iron-giant-disciple-dna-vip/

It would not be right for me to mention King Lion on this list of legends without mentioning his legendary son, ICK's Disciple. Disciple was even *larger* than his father, the great King Lion. Disciple was also more well-known than King Lion, as he ended up landing a spot in the famous reality television series, *The Real Housewives Of Orange County.*

Disciple was the production of one of my mentors, Roman Vaughn. Roman bred his female Q-Ball to King Lion, the legend himself. Disciple carried a sinister look and was the size of a beast. King Lion truly outproduced himself and proved himself as a super-producer in his own right. Disciple went on to consistently produce both male and female offspring just as impressive as himself. My first breeding ever was with Disciple, but that is not the reason I believe he deserved a spot on this list. His impact on the BGK bloodline has nothing to do with the reason why he is deemed a legend. It is due to his overall impact on the XL American Bully community as a whole. Everybody in the community knows of him and his productions.

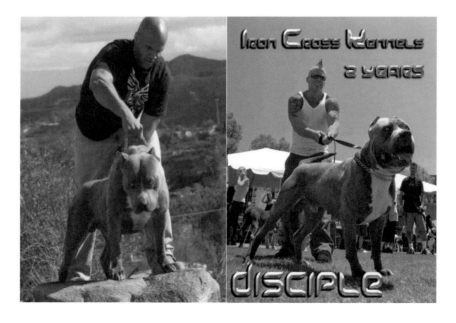

Due to Roman's powerful marketing and Disciple's

infamous show appearances, more people ended up recognizing Disciple than King Lion. As a result, he ended up surpassing his dad in popularity and notoriety. When people saw Disciple in person they could not believe how good he looked. His head shape and sheer stature simply left crowds in awe. It seemed as though everybody in the Bully community wanted a chance to have a Disciple of their own as a premier stud for their kennel. Sadly, Roman got banned from the UKC for falsifying documentation and registering a litter as Disciple's which actually belonged to another stud. Disciple had an undeniably tremendous impact on the XL American Bully community, and we are very grateful for his lasting legacy.

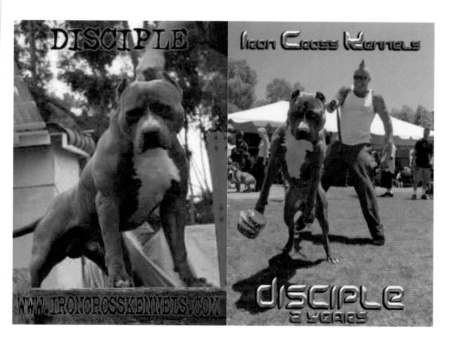

DISCIPLE

5. Arnold the Terminator of NIS

Pedigree: https://www.pitpedia.com/dog/nis-arnold-the-terminator-dna-p/

This Bully legend was purchased and owned by Kat of Bossy Kennels. Although Arnold was already in the makings of being a legend before she bought him, she helped to take him to that next level. Kat's marketing genius led to this dog's ascent to legendary status. His look gained him a lot of attention in the community due to his overdone muscular build. They called him "The Terminator" for good reason, even his muscles had muscles! On top of that, he looked even better in person. People wanted a dog like Arnold, and one with his impressively chiseled frame as well. They would've been happy to have his name in their pedigree. He was a very impressive dog, who left a lasting impact on the community and lived long past his years. Whenever Arnold showed up at the dog shows, people were blown away by his physique in person. He had the stature of a bulky bodybuilder in the form of an amazing XL American Bully. Arnold also was an amazing producer creating incredible offspring with the same traits that he carried.

6. Lor's Blue Terminator (aka Comet or Juice) of Extreme Bully Kennels

Pedigree: https://www.pitpedia.com/dog/lors-blue-terminator/

Comet was a very impressive dog, and one of the founding dogs that set the standard of how an XL American Bully should look. He was one of the main dogs to put the true essence of Bully into the game. His wide build, thick neck, massive head, and serious look/drive were what inspired many breeders and dog enthusiasts during this time. He was owned by Eddie Lor of Extreme Bully Kennels (XBK). Eddie marketed him very well, leading Comet to become a great producer with a public following. He is another super-producer that had a significant effect on the Bully community. I am proud to say his name can be found in some of my pedigrees.

One of his most famous offspring is a stud named XB's Icon, who was also owned by XBK. Comet was commonly called "The Juice" because everyone wanted to use him as a stud for their own program, so his semen was highly sought after. Eddie, however, tended to keep the dog exclusive and did not breed him out to just anyone, thus making him sought after all the more. He was a great step forward for the Bully community. People assume because I have a large, high-end home that it can act as an invitation, but that is not the case for me. I am a very private person. I will meet my clients at the local park where they can interact with my dogs, but I do not have them come to my home. However, Eddie was quite different from me in that aspect. He used to always tell me, "Dre, you have a big beautiful million dollar home, a pool, a waterfall, and a huge yard. You need to have your clients come over it and enjoy it with you".

Eddie constantly allowed his clients to party in his upscale home and know his location. This ultimately led to two men in masks arriving on his property and trying to kick in his front door and failing. As the two would-be robbers attempted to kick in his door, Eddie got on his John Wick sh**

and turned into an assassin on a mission. Eddie looked through his peephole to locate the position of the robbers, and shot one of the men through his door, striking him center mass and leaving him dead on the front porch. The other robber bolted away from the crime scene, and would later turn himself in for the attempted crime. The few in the Bully community that found out what had happened were completely surprised that Eddie Lor was even capable of this at all considering that he was a soft-spoken, well-mannered Asian man who didn't curse. You never know what someone is truly capable of until they are placed in a life or death situation. On a side note, Eddie ended up going from breeding XL American Bullies to Frenchies, and although I wish he didn't, what can you do? I understand why he did it, no judgment on this end. I often get asked why I do not invite my clients to my home. This is exactly why I choose to not engage in such a dangerous practice in this current crazy world. Returning to the topic at hand, Comet has a long-standing impact on the XL American Bully community. Many breeders today are still trying to achieve the same look that he had, as he was a very wide and massive dog. His stature was incredibly impressive and his legacy is undeniable

7. The Rock of Big Gemini Kennels - aka "BGK's The Rock"

Pedigree: https://www.pitpedia.com/dog/bgks-the-rock/

Anyone who knows me, knows that this dog is near and dear to my heart, and he was one of the best friends I've had in my life, but that is not the reason he is on this list. He is on this list because he truly deserves his spot. Even though he was known worldwide as BGK's The Rock, his registered name with the UKC was Sunlines Gladiator Rock. He was produced by Anthony Sun of Sunline Kennels, and I purchased him as a young adult. Due to my understanding of marketing, and Rock's incredible stature and look, I was able to make him a world-famous superstar. To be honest, Rock was a superstar in his own right, I was just the lucky guy holding the leash and spoiling him like the King that he was. He was everything that a breeder could hope for when it came to XL American Bullies.

If you want to talk about temperament, size, structure, movement, longevity (considering that he lived to be roughly 13.5 years old), and his insane production power, not many dogs of any breed can compete with him. The Rock has produced some legends of his own, one of which was BGK's

Cujo. Rock's lineage is full of greatness, and his notoriety as a worldwide superstar will be his regal legacy in the XL American Bully history books. His grandfather was the amazing legend Juan Gotty, and his father is the legendary honorable mention "Reyes' Stone." BGK's The Rock was Reyes Stone's largest and most legendary son. Rock was very popular with the general public, and if you remember what was stated earlier, being involved in mainstream media holds heavy importance when it comes to the XL American Bully breed. He made an indelible paw print on the concrete foundation of American Bully history. His impact upon the general public solidified his legacy as a true XL American Bully legend. Multiple videos which were posted on the Big Gemini Kennels Youtube channel generated viral numbers, up in the millions, including his infamous Service Dog videos. The videos were so popular and gained so much traction that BGK's The Rock ended up being posted by Worldstar Hip-Hop as their animal clip of the week, and that was without my knowledge or permission. Rock's video did over two million views in one day on Worldstarhiphop,

https://worldstarhiphop.com/videos/video.php?v=wshhZM8cjmKc6Zx9MBsO

His impact can be seen by the number of people he was able to inspire to join the XL American Bully movement. He used to be titled "The World's Largest Pitbull" due to people's misunderstanding of the Bully breed vs Pitbulls. To be clear, BGK's The Rock was an XL American Bully. Rock's viral YouTube videos were seen globally and were even translated into different languages, going viral in the Spanish market as well. I allowed him to interact with people at public locations so that people could become more educated about the XL American Bully breed. BGK's The Rock was a super-producer who ended up outproducing himself time and time again. The same thing happened with BGK's Cujo, BGK's Debo, BGK's Azore, BGK's New York, BGK's Magnum, BGk's Picasso, etc. The Rock was so influential in the American Bully movement that he was the forerunner to other famed XL American Bullies who followed after him. BGK's The Rock's fame was the precursor to the rise of DDK's The Hulk, who followed his paw prints as a viral internet XL American Bully sensation. His widespread marketing and unprecedented production power undeniably played a significant role in the XL American Bully world, and greatly increased public awareness, and brought even more interest in the breed. Simply put, BGK's The Rock converted a staggering amount of people into American Bully fans.

8. BGK's Cujo of Big Gemini Kennels

Pedigree: https://www.pitpedia.com/dog/bgks-cujo/

The infamous BGK's Cujo, son of BGK's The Rock, was undeniably another XL American Bully legend. He was first marketed and became well known in the United States, but he fully matured and obtained international fame after I sold him to a client in Europe and established BGK Europe to represent my kennel overseas. BGK's Cujo became wildly popular after being the first XL American Bully to break into the international market. Simply put, he was the first known XL American Bully in Europe.

BGK's CUJO

When he arrived, I was able to establish BGK Europe and my international partners became overnight celebrities because of the immense popularity of BGK's Cujo. They had only seen true American pitbull terriers before Cujo's arrival. We created a new market in the European community as a result of his XL muscular structure, and impressively unique look. BGK's Cujo was such a phenomenon that from the moment he arrived in Europe, people would knock on the door of the new co-owners just to see him in person, and he did not even know these people! We still don't know how people came to find out which house Cujo was going to! If you were to look at the pedigrees of the dogs within Europe's XL American Bully community, you would see BGK Cujo's name all over the ABKC & EBKC registry.

BGK's Cujo and his litter! Super Producer II

BGK's Cujo instantly became a household name in Europe. BGK Europe and I along with ABKC/EBKC Judge Ragim Simone Magh hosted the first XL American Bully dog show called the BGK Bday, and tons of people showed up from all over Europe to attend. I appeared at the show virtually via Skype on the big screen and it was amazing to see the crowd staring at me, hanging on my every word, which was being translated to them. BGK's The Rock and BGKs

42

Cujo's influence was undeniable. Take a look at that video here from our first European American Bully show: https://youtu.be/kK1la2ZMFFE. BGK's Cujo single-handedly launched the American Bully movement which began in Europe, The Netherlands, The UK, and beyond thus helping to spread greater interest in the XL American Bully breed.

On the left is my good friend and business partner the founder of BGK Europe, Patrick Fernald, and on the right is my good friend ABKC/EBKC Judge Ragim Magh:

Without him, Europe would not be as into XL Bullies as they are now. Before BGK's Cujo and BGK's The Rock, these sizes were practically unheard of! This breed needed the push that Cujo was able to provide for it to be able to create its roots and strengthen its foundation. The fact that BGK's Cujo consistently outproduced himself from the very first litter to his most recent was also incredibly impressive. BGK's Cujo's production power was the only thing that was more impressive than his looks. BGK's Cujo's sons ranged from 140-200 lbs carrying a very definitive beautiful look. BGK's Shadow, BGK's Tank, BGK's Trex, and BGK's El Turbo, were among his most amazing productions and the list goes on and on and on and...etc. You get the picture. BGK's Cujo was undeniably a super producer, so Europe was spoiled from their very first taste of true XL American Bully. BGK's Cujo is

44

an undisputed American Bully Legend and one of my favorite

BGK's CUJO,
We breed for temperament!

dogs to ever walk the planet. I truly wish I had never sold him, but it did greatly advance the breed.

Rest In Peace
LEGEND
Big Gemini Kennels

BGK'S
CUJO
3-10-2009 - JULY 1 2020

9. Show Stoppin' ACE, (aka ACE), of Top Dog Kennels

Pedigree: https://www.pitpedia.com/dog/next-levels-show-stoppin-ace/

The amazing American Bully known as Ace was produced by Next Level Kennels, but owned by Top Dog Kennels. He was such an incredibly built dog that he took the entire American Bully world by storm. Ace was a beautiful dog with an impeccable structure, and his offspring were just as stunning. One of his most notable productions was a female by the name of Victoria's Secret, a chiseled dam owned by Bossy Kennels. She is one of the most beautiful XL American Bully females I have ever laid eyes on.

Here is the picture of Victorias Secret that has gone viral multiple times because of her impressively unique physique.

Another Ace production that was owned by Bossy Kennels was a male named Adios, who was also a stunning dog as well. Due to Bossy Kennels' tenacious marketing campaign, these dogs ended up being *very* well known. Ace would attend dog shows where he would be stacked up next to dogs who were larger than himself, but because of his spectacular build and stature, he would win the stack off not because he was bigger, but because he was better looking and embodied that elusive X-factor. For those who do not know, a stack-off is a competition where you put two dogs side by side, and compare the two, while you judge and choose which one you prefer. For example, when Ace was stacked next to AIP's Moron, he dominated him and was the clear choice that he was the more complete bull. Check out Top Dog Kennels, as they continue to produce beasts from Ace's bloodline. Ace is considered a Super Producer because of his amazing offspring. He consistently outproduced himself and became among the most highly sought-after bloodlines to have in a top-quality pedigree.

10. King Kong (aka KONG) of Pro Bull Kennels

Pedigree: https://www.pitpedia.com/dog/pro-bulls-king-kong/

There is no other way to describe Kong other than a legendary beast. His origins can be traced back to ICK, as Roman was the producer of Kong's father, Moron, (he would go on to be the best offspring that Moron had ever created). King Kong represented the future of size because he was not only big, but wide. To me, XBK's Comet brought the standard of wide Bullies to the XL American Bully community. However, King Kong brought huge size *and* girth. He was yet another super-producer, who created several show-stopping beasts with a uniquely identifiable look. Simply put, Kong's offspring are very easy to identify. When Kong was producing, he was a stud in high demand, and all anyone could talk about!

Kong left an indelible imprint on the Bully community by the way he changed people's views on Bullies and helped them to determine what type of style they would like to have in their yard. People wanted the super-sized girth and width that Kong displayed, and they still do. His lineage is still being continued to this day, and even now, you can still see his physical traits being carried on via his grandchildren and great children. Impressive!

11. UKC's Most Wanted Kimbo

Pedigree: https://www.pitpedia.com/dog/ukcs-most-wanted-kimbo/

Kimbo has earned his rightful place on this list by being another super-producer. He created great-looking dogs with incredible structure, solid masses, and solid domes. While his offspring may have bodies that sit a little lower to the ground, they were able to make up for it with their girth, head size, and overall shape. If you were looking for a fawn mid-sized XL American Bully, you were most certainly going after Kimbo's bloodline. Kimbo carried a thick neck, short snout, bulky head, and short back along with the width/girth that the American Bully world loves. Kimbo consistently reproduced and outproduced himself, breeding after breeding. **However,**

Kimbo does have a controversial past in the XL Bully world since some of his direct offspring were known to be far too H.A. (human-aggressive). Kimbo's offspring have attacked and injured multiple innocent people, and even have gone as far as killing multiple people both children and elderly, (may the victims rest in peace). https://www.nola.com/news/politics/article_1842471f-f06c-5d97-aa70-adf09193b749.html. I will say that as far as I know, the majority of his offspring have not been randomly human aggressive, only about 20% of his offspring had this deadly undesired horrific genetic character trait. https://www.dailymail.co.uk/news/article-2601672/130lb-monster-pit-bull-killed-owners-daughter-four-inbred.html. I do not condone or breed randomly human-aggressive dogs. I have only ever had one dog in my yard who had Kimbo in his pedigree which was from multiple generations back.

KIMBO BLOODLINE
XL BULLY PRODUCER

That being said, I felt the need to include Kimbo, (dark controversy aside), because he still had an enduring impact on the XL American Bully breed. The Kimbo line, despite its ignominious history, has created some notable offspring, one of which is his son, Juggernaut. That dog had it all! While I have criticized this dog in the past due to his aggressive line, I do have to be fair and include him in this list of American Bully legends whether I like it or not; his history and powerful impact can never be erased from the XL American Bully world.

UKC'S MOST WANTED KIMBO

12. UKC's The Unstoppable Juggernaut

Pedigree: https://www.pitpedia.com/dog/the-unstopable-juggernaut/

Since we have discussed his father, Kimbo, I found it only fitting to include his legendary bull of a son in this list as well. Juggernaut gave a new definition to the word "freak" to the Bully community. This was around the time when people were chasing after what was commonly referred to as the "freak factor" in their dogs. People wanted a more low-profile beefy XL American Bully and extremely wide at the same time. Juggernaut had that factor to the extreme. He had what the people wanted, and he left them wanting even more. His build was *extra* wide with a *super* large dome and he was big-boned all at the same time. A lot of pedigrees proudly claim Juggernaut's name in their program because he was a heavily desired stud, which produced dogs with a similar structure to himself, thus becoming a super producer in the process.

Much like his father, he made a significant impact on the XL American Bully community. It was truly an awe-inspiring sight to see the way that dog properly carried his weight. He made an impression not only on me, but the entire XL Bully world! So if you are looking to discuss Bully history, then you can not discuss it without talking about Juggernaut and his father.

13. De La Cruz's Escalade 5150 (aka Escalade)

Pedigree: https://www.pitpedia.com/dog/dela-cruzs-escalade-5150-dna-p/

While Escalade was not only a huge contributor to the XL American Bully community for both his size and look, he also had an interesting backstory. When I first heard of Escalade, he was owned by Boss Up Kennels' Matt, (one of my

OG mentors who helped get me informed when I started in the breeding game). I first learned about the dog through Roman, who had told me at the time that it would not be a good idea to breed to Escalade as he might be a mixed breed, (Presa Canario). Flash forward to when I bought BGK's The Rock, Roman began to switch up and was starting to praise and use Escalade as a stud *immediately* after. Kind of odd, don't you think? Personally, I know that Roman must have been scared, knowing that I was going to out-produce him because he ended up breeding the same dog that he claimed to be a "mixed breed" to *every* female that came into heat in his yard during that time period!

This was when Escalade truly made his mark and where Moron, Stalefish, Excalibur, etc. all came to existence as a result of these sporadically desperate breedings. If you notice, all of these amazing dogs were produced by Roman around the same time. However, to Escalade's credit, he was a damn good producer considering he produced AIP's Moron who ended up being the father of Probulls' King Kong, who is also on this very legends list. Stalefish and Excalibur ended up being amazing producers as well. I actually own an Excalibur daughter myself, and I am very proud of her size/and temperament. She loves family but will literally terminate any trespasser on site. In his latter years, after Escalade had made a name for himself, he was sold to Tyler Long, owner of Triple Cross Kennels.

This is where he would spend his final years. Unfortunately, Tyler of TCK had to quit breeding after being caught with 250 pounds of marijuana with a California deputy guarding his large marijuana shipment somewhere on the east coast. I couldn't believe it! See the story here: https://www.mintpressnews.com/california-deputy-caught-with-250lbs-pounds-of-marijuana/212473/

14. DDK's The Hulk

Pedigree: https://www.pitpedia.com/dog/ddk9s-the-hulk/

The Hulk happens to be the only dog on this list who is still alive, which makes him the only living legend! Some of the honorable mentions are alive, but all other listed legends are no longer with us. DDK's The Hulk is a household name, and this is not me being biased, he has rightfully earned his spot in the XL American Bully Hall Of Fame. He too has been given the same title by the masses enjoyed by the late great BGK's The Rock. DDK's The Hulk was also deemed "The World's Largest Pitbull". According to our previously stated clarification of Pitbulls vs Bullies, he should be defined as *one* of the largest XL American Bullies. Even though he is not the largest XL American Bully out there, he is one of the most marketed. Furthermore, DDK's The Hulk is the only known XL American Bully with a household name, verified Instagram account with over 1 million followers (and growing), millions of Youtube views, a highly successful family show on YouTube, and has even made appearances on Good Morning America, The View, and several magazine issues worldwide.

Hulk, 175-Pound Pit Bull Visits The View

Unfortunately, mainstream media became obsessed with Hulk as "The World's Largest Pitbull" instead of what he actually is, a huge XL American Bully. Despite being mislabeled, DDK's The Hulk has become a natural phenomenon and has brought greater interest and visibility to this beloved breed. Marlon Grennan, the owner and producer of DDK's The Hulk, has helped bring the emerging breed into the public spotlight. This is very helpful because when you have a breed as new and emerging as the XL American Bully, you're going to need breed ambassadors like Marlon who will help pave the way. The Hulk has some great offspring as well such as DDK's Kong, (not related to the one discussed previously on this list), DDK's Kobe, BGK's Coco, CBK's Willow, and many others. While a lot of people try to downplay the impact that DDK's The Hulk had on the XL Bully community, it is undeniable. The fact that he is a household name to the general public who are outside of the Bully community is enough in itself to prove The Hulk's lasting impact upon the world and the XL American Bully breed. He is a true breed ambassador and an American Bully legend.

15. Mugleston's Blue Boogie Monster (aka Boogie)

Pedigree: https://www.pitpedia.com/dog/muglestons-conan/

Mugleston's Boogie was born in 2003, right before the American Bully Kennel Club was officially formed. Keep in mind, this was when the breed was just getting both established and accepted by the ABKC. It barely had its footing when Boogie burst onto the scene. Before I even had my website or thought about breeding, Boogie was already making a name for himself. Everybody, and I mean *everybody*, wanted to get offspring from him. He was such an impressive blue brolic beast of a dog. The Bully community loved him!

He became a recognized name the same way that the DDK's The Hulk did, and this was before there were different types of social media platforms to promote yourself/or your dog. Blue Boogie Monster's productions were just as impressive as he was. Therefore, he has earned legendary status due to his lasting impact on the XL Bully community and his amazing production power, which he was able to showcase when the breed became established.

16. ICK's Iron Tyson DNA-P

Pedigree: https://www.pitpedia.com/dog/iron-cross-iron-tyson-dna-p/

This majestic blue beast of an XL American Bully was the first that I ever had the pleasure of viewing in person. He was owned by my mentor, Roman Vaughn of Iron Cross Kennels. Iron Tyson helped to set the stage for big athletic American Bullies with both his serious drive and amazing production power. Back when I was first browsing through different kennels websites so that I could pick where I wanted to purchase my foundation stock from, I came across this amazing stud. Upon seeing him, I instantly knew that he would be the one to provide me with the foundation for my program. He proved himself to be one of the original super-producers, creating top-quality males and females, production after production. What's even more impressive is, his productions were able to produce the same style, look, and temperament as their infamous father. Iron Tyson was a true alpha male and not for the weak. He produced amazing specimens such as ICK's Iron Maiden, (see picture below), who was a female that looked better than most males!

Another amazing female Iron Tyson produced that had a fire drive, insane structure, and muscles was ICK's Iron Pride,

Iron Tyson was able to consistently produce the original APBT look and temperament on a super-sized frame. In his prime, he was one of the most sought-after and influential studs in the XL American Bully world! He consistently produced what I considered, "Super-Sized Pitbulls", and when I incorporated his blood into my program, it allowed me to create monsters such as BGK's T-Rex, Tank, etc., who carried his looks on a 163+ lb frame. There is no denying that he is a true XL American Bully legend.

17. Coleone's King

Pedigree: https://www.pitpedia.com/dog/coleone-kennels-king/

Coleone's King was a beautiful tri-bully who had a *crazy* impact on the XL breed and created tremendous productions. Bossy Kennels, among others, has used him frequently for top-quality breedings. He produced XL beauties such as the legendary Markoff, Sin City's Bellagio (another one of our honorable mentions), and a host of other amazing dogs. If you look through the pedigrees within the XL American Bully community, (especially with dogs that have color), you're likely to find King's name on the paperwork, as he had highly sought-after blood. Kat of Bossy Kennels made a very wise business move by breeding with King early on and adding his bloodline to her yard and creating Bossy's Willy Wonka, father of Bossy's Goodbar. The same goes for Sin City Kennels and any other kennel that I did not mention that used his blood too. Coleone's King proved to the American Bully community, production after production, that he was an amazing producer! His impact on the XL American Bully breed is not only irrefutable, but legendary.

18. Primeyard's Mr. Markoff

Pedigree: https://www.pitpedia.com/dog/primeyards-mr-markoff/

Now, this dog may be viewed as controversial to some people as they do not believe that he has done enough to properly earn his spot among the legends. Sadly, he was not able to fully show his capabilities as he did not get to live a full life. However, when I had discussed this dog with my peers prior to curating this list, some of them had stated that they personally viewed him as an undeniable legend. So the opinions on this dog may differ depending on who you are conversing with. Markoff was a big-boned tri-colored XL American Bully and the most well-known son of the legend: Coleone's King, (previously mentioned). He carried the "heavy bone and big dome structure" that the Bully community wanted to see not in only the common XL American Bullies but the tri-colored Bullies as well.

Even till this day, his bloodline is still highly valuable and sought-after. Which makes sense because Markoff was a beautiful specimen and an even better producer! So much so, that he was able to peak greater interest in the tri-colored XL American Bullies. However, people were still afraid to "try the tri", (get it?). Markoff was able to make it possible for people to see that you can still have a beautiful tri-coat on a dog without sacrificing an incredible weight and size on them. Whether or not Markoff is more of a legend or an honorable mention, is up to you to decide. At the end of the day, he was unquestionably a great producer and an overall spectacular specimen of an American Bully.

19. Die Hard Straight Out of Compton aka Mac-10

Pedigree: https://www.pitpedia.com/dog/diehard-straight-outta-compton/

Mac-10 was one of the freakiest American Bullies to walk the planet. Both his bone and width were super impressive. Not only did Mac-10 stop traffic with his compact, low-to-the-ground stature, XL wide frame, and incredible headpiece, but he also consistently produced and outproduced himself time after time.

Mac-10's popularity quickly grew in the American Bully community. When he attended dog shows, he did not need to go into the show ring in order to impress the crowd. In fact, it was quite the opposite. The spectators and dog lovers alike would create a ring around him because his mere presence demanded attention. Saul Cervantes of Royal Blue Generation decided to purchase Mac-10 after being impressed by the way this dog was developing, producing, and quickly becoming an icon within the Bully community. Once Saul took custody of Mac-10, his popularity sky-rocketed even further as well as his productions. Mac-10 had clicked extremely well with the RBG females he was bred with and began producing *huge* freaky monsters back to back. Some of his more notable productions include: Die Hard's Iron Tank,

Blue Line's Mack Tenna 2007, RBG's Sniper, etc. Mac-10 left an enduring legacy upon the American Bully community and is, without a doubt, an XL American Bully legend.

20. Fireline's Knocks-ville

Pedigree: https://www.pitpedia.com/dog/firelines-knocks-ville/

Fireline's Knocks-ville represented his kennel's name with his fiery disposition and shredded frame. He was very similar to his father, the legendary Iron Tyson, when it came to having an extremely strong drive as well as being one of the most athletic XL American Bullies on this legendary list. From hitting the spring pole to being a fearless guardian who protected his family with every inch of being, and even being able to run full speed for extreme distances. Knocks also turned out to be an incredible producer just like his father, passing on his drive/temperament, along with his muscle tone, and his athletic abilities to his offspring consistently. Although Knocks was labeled an XL American Bully, I viewed him as a super-sized American pitbull terrier at heart as well as his offspring. These were dogs that needed a truly alpha owner who was capable of handling a high-energy super-sized beast of a dog. Fireline's Knocks was one of the dogs that convinced the community that the XL American Bully can still be a working dog capable of hunting, protection work, and any other high-energy efforts. When you saw Knocks-ville in person, you would surely perceive him as a supersized APBT. He was truly an XL American Bully legend that heavily influenced the community.

Legendary Honorable Mentions

Our honorable mentions list includes dogs that hold legendary status. While they are not *fully* legends, they have made a significant impact on the XL American Bully breed, making a difference as they were introduced to the scene. At the time when this book was written, a lot of these incredible dogs are still alive and producing, or have recently passed.

1. Bossy Kennels, Mr. Goodbar

Pedigree: https://www.pitpedia.com/dog/bossys-mr-goodbar/

Our first honorable mention is Bossy Kennels, Mr. Goodbar. He's an impressive chocolate tri XL American Bully, who has influenced many kennels and produced several beasts. When you talk about overall size, structure, look, "x-factor", or anything you wanted in a tri, Mr. Goodbar has it! Presently, he is quite influential in the XL American Bully market and will continue to be, as he is a super-producer and a well-structured stud with a coveted pedigree and is extremely popular as were his predecessors, who both reached legendary status, Markoff and King Coleone. These two great studs were the father and grandfather of Goodbar, so his legendary production power shouldn't be much of a

surprise to anyone that understands a top-quality XL American Bully pedigree. Bossy Kennels has a winner with this boy!

Here is Mr. Goodbar with the celebrity known as "Dancing Dan" aka Dan Rue of Nick Cannon's Wild N Out Television show.

2. Daniel Reyes' Stone

Pedigree: https://www.pitpedia.com/dog/reyes-stone/

Our second honorable mention is going to be Daniel Reyes' Stone. If you recall, Stone was mentioned earlier when we discussed his face-off picture with King Lion, which clearly showed he was a larger beast than the legend King Lion. The Bully community agreed that Stone definitely stood out in that picture; He held stunning physical traits such as a *huge* blocky head, wide chest, great topline, and a fiery temperament to match. What a beast of an XL American Bully! Now while there is no such thing as a true XXL

American Bully, I believe that if there were then Stone would be the foundation stud, as I would call him, the "Dog Father". When you talk about XL Blue Bullies, Stone deserves his credit as being the blueprint for being a true XL super-producer. Stone out-produced himself with BGK's The Rock and his siblings. The entire litter was HUGE! Defying all odds, BGK's The Rock developed into an even larger version of his father. In order to further prove that his father was a true super-producer, BGK's The Rock, like his father, would go on to produce even larger versions of himself with an even better structure time and time again. Production power clearly transfers from generation to generation, with this incredible genetic pool. I am truly blessed to have it presently running strong in the BGK program.

Unfortunately, Stone died at a young age due to a spider bite and did not get to contribute as much to the community in order to prove himself as I know he could have. Luckily, I had the honor of owning his son as my foundation stud before his untimely passing. The fact that he produced BGK's The Rock, who then produced BGK's Cujo, who then went on to produce BGK's T-Rex, is enough to prove that Stone could have been a legend if he had lived long enough.

In this infamous picture, the legendary Stone is on the right and he is faced-off with the famous Bully Remy Martin at a dog show. Once again the fiery beast Stone appears to be the larger Bully in this picture, and is not backing down. Stone is an American Bully legend who died prematurely before he was able to make it to legendary status.

3. Blueline's Smokie, The Mexican Ghost-face Assassin, aka "Blueline's Smokie"

Pedigree:https://www.pitpedia.com/dog/bluelines-smokie-the-mexican-ghost-face-assasin/

This is what happens when you combine two legends into one pedigree. Blueline's Smokie's father was the legendary King Lion, and his mother was LOMELI'S DA HOODRAT BLUELINE, a daughter of the legendary West Side Monster. What an amazing pedigree!

Our third honorable mention is Blueline's Smokey (aka Ghostface). He was another King Lion's son who did a lot for the XL Bully community and was well marketed by Eddie of Blueline Kennels. Smokie had a classically beautiful look to him. When he went to dog shows, there would be large cutout images of him with large crowds encompassing him. Everyone loved him! When he was still in the game, people were desperate for productions from Smokie. It was alleged that Smokie only had one testicle, but one thing is for sure, he had true production power and a legendary pedigree. If anything, only having one testicle makes him all the more remarkable!

You can find him in pictures with famous rappers in the music industry such as this picture with DJ Quik & Kurupt, two West Coast Hip Hop legends in their own right.

Therefore, Smokie deserves an honorable mention due to the imprint that he left behind in the XL American Bully community. The way that Eddie promoted Smokie deserves to be recognized as well because it helped to add to his influence. Smokie's place in XL American Bully history books is beyond question. Without him and his incredible production power, (as well as a stacked pedigree), there are a lot of kennels that would not exist considering the fact that they built it with his offspring as their foundation. The way that Eddie was able to integrate the Hip-Hop community with the XL American Bully community helped to tie the two worlds together, and I have to give credit to him, it was a genius marketing technique.

4. Steelhead's Giant Q-Ball aka "ICK's Q-Ball"

Pedigree: https://www.pitpedia.com/dog/steelheads-giant-q-ball-dna-p/

Our fourth honorable mention is Steelhead's Giant Q-Ball, the only female mentioned in this book. She was the only female I have seen who could super-size everything that she touched. Her production power was truly amazing, proving herself time after time. When she was bred to King Lion, she created Disciple, and the pattern would continue on from there. Roman received an incredible producer in Q- Ball, and she easily made XL American Bully history. Everybody wanted offspring from her the same way they desired offspring from other legendary males because the community knew that if you bred to ICK's Q- Ball, you were likely to end up with something even bigger. She had an incredible impact during her reign as the "Queen of Iron Cross Kennels" and has rightfully earned her spot in XL American Bully history.

5. RBG's King Liger

Pedigree: https://www.pitpedia.com/dog/royal-bloodlines-king-liger/

Our fifth honorable mention is RBG's King Liger, yet another King Lion son. He had the ability to stop shows without even getting into the show ring! The crowds at the show would create a ring around him! He carried the size, the neck, the drive, the movement, and the alpha-ness about him that everyone loved, myself included. His only downfall was that he was not able to create offspring that were either at the same level as him or better. He tended to produce dogs who were typically smaller than his size. Liger's better productions were female rather than his male offspring. Regardless, the breed type, structure, muscle, and athleticism could all still be seen. One of his more notable productions is Blackmail who is currently owned by Kat of Bossy Kennels, and she keeps him as her house dog. I bred him myself using BGK's Big Sexy, (a sister of BGK's Cujo), and he produced an amazing litter for me. Although he typically threw smaller males with other females, in my BGK litter he produced some undeniable *monster* males! Here is one of the males from my breeding with him called BGK's King Buddy. Maybe he just needed the right bloodline to click with.

King Liger was so impressive that video footage of him just running around his yard roughhousing with his owner's friend Billy has generated millions of views. Here's the infamous clip: https://youtu.be/6PCmg7oZtEY

6. Sin City Bullies' Bellagio

Pedigree: https://www.pitpedia.com/dog/sincitybullies-bellagio/

Our sixth honorable mention is Sin City's Bellagio, owned by Kazon Thomas. He is consistently producing beautiful Bully XL American tri-bullies. Bellagio is a problem, and as an American Bully connoisseur I am very selective when it comes to saying such things, but it's true for this dog. He is incredible in every sense of the word. Bellagio has a dark and beautiful look as well as an excellent head shape. As the son of the legendary Coleone's King, it could be said that he has amazing blood in him from the start. My friends over at the Incredibullz kennel are currently using his bloodline, and I have to say, I love what I am seeing! I can't wait to see what he goes on to produce! If you haven't checked this boy out yet, you need to, because not only is he very impressive, he is constantly reproducing and out-producing himself every breeding. This amazing specimen as well as his productions deserve much more recognition than they are currently receiving.

7. XB Lor's Bully Icon aka "Icon"

Pedigree: https://www.pitpedia.com/dog/xb-lors-bully-icon/

Our seventh honorable mention is XB's Bully Icon (aka Icon), the son of XB's Comet. Icon was appropriately named considering that he was, in fact, an icon in the Bully community. He was one of the legends of XB's Comet's top productions, and he also had the legend, Juan Gotty, in his pedigree as well. Icon had a beautiful wide chest, big bones, flashy markings, and that "wow-factor" that is still greatly sought-after in the XL American Bully community. He carried the ideal phenotype and genotype that is highly sought-after to this day by breeders and buyers alike. He was so impressive that he would shut down shows when he appeared in person. While he wasn't too tall, his girth was just perfect, making what the community calls a "true bull". If you ask me, Icon had a better front than his father. I even used an Icon daughter myself, Lil' Diva, in my breeding program and pedigrees, as he is BGK's Picasso's grandfather. People still seek out his type of build to this day! The *only* reason XB's Icon is on the honorable mention list, instead of the legends list is because he could not reproduce or out-produce himself when bred. Everyone wanted their own version of Icon, but he didn't have his father's legendary production power, unfortunately. Nonetheless, he was still iconic (pun intended).

8. SIK's Grand Champ Caribou Lou

Pedigree:<u>https://www.pitpedia.com/dog/siks-caribou-lou/</u>

Our eighth honorable mention is SIK's Grand Champ "Caribou Lou", who was an ABKC Grand champion, (hence the title in his name). This boy was the truth! He was a big fawn dog with an incredible build on him, and his head size was so extreme they had to measure it in public for the non-believers. I believe his head measured roughly 27 and a half inches. He was the only dog within the entirety of this list who held multiple champion titles. This shows that he was able to prove himself both in and out of the show ring, as he was a great producer. When people saw him in person, or at the shows, they could not believe the beast before them. This dog was a sight to behold! He was crowned as the "largest head" at multiple Bully shows. Overall this legendary Bully impressed judges at the dog shows, as well as the American Bully community.

9. BGK's Shadow

Pedigree:https://www.pitpedia.com/dog/pr-bgk-europes-shadow/

Our ninth honorable mention is BGK's Shadow, currently owned by Manmade Kennels but produced by BGK Europe, as he is the son of the legend: BGK's Cujo. He was actually the first offspring that Cujo had ever produced in Europe, and it was an impressive production through and through. He quickly rose to stardom in Europe, dominating shows and crowds alike. BGK's Shadow became an overnight superstar once imported to the USA by Eddie of Manmade Kennels. When you look at BGK's Shadow, he is everything you would want to see in an XL American Bully beast. He's super thick with a wide head, blocky shoulders, and chest. He has an amazing temperament to match and is great around kids. He lacks in no areas! Shadow has definitely been able to prove himself so far as an incredible producer, due to his consistent creations that are just as good or better than himself. Some of his offspring have become champions in the show ring. Since he has been at Manmade Kennels, he has gained much more exposure on social media and is becoming increasingly famous within the XL American Bully community in both the United States and Europe. Shoutout to Manmade's Eddie for giving him the attention and recognition he truly deserves!

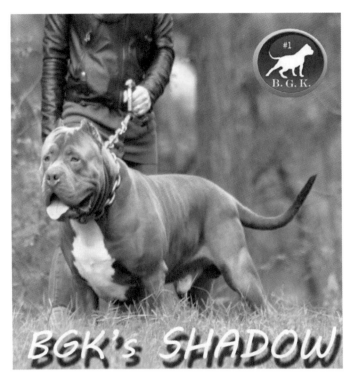

BGK's SHADOW

Can BGK's Cujo produce?!

10. BGK's Tank

Pedigree:https://www.pitpedia.com/dog/bgks-tank/

Our tenth honorable mention is BGK's Tank, another product of legendary BGK's Cujo. Tank was a true super-producer, proven by both reproducing and outproducing himself multiple times. Some of his pups grew up to become renowned champions in the show ring. When he attended dog shows he ended up weighing in at 167 pounds in front of the entire amazed audience! He would shut down dog shows that he attended due to the overwhelming attention he received because of his massive size. One outstanding accomplishment achieved by BGK's Tank was that he was featured in a film starring both Keanu Reeves and Ana De Armas entitled "Exposed".

This was great exposure for both Tank and the XL American Bully breed! I have to give a hand to Paul of Top Blue Kennels for his amazing job in raising and marketing this

impressive dog. BGK's blood is undeniably powerful, and continues to be generation after generation!

BGK's Tank was the third pick. Here is the super impressive brother: BGK's T-Rex, another Cujo son!

11. BGK's Debo

Pedigree: https://www.pitpedia.com/dog/bgks-debo/

BGK's Debo is truly a great representation of his father, the legendary BGK's The Rock. BGK's Debo is a product of BGK's The Rock bred to his daughter BGK's Lyric, and is a larger version of his father, sitting at 163 lbs. BGK's The Rock weighed in at 150 lbs. BGK's Debo has everything the community loves about an XL American Bully: big bones, big dome, great topline, great structure, strong rear, wide chest, and overall a very intimidating look. BGK's Debo also carries his father's well-balanced temperament and most importantly his legendary production power. BGK's Debo has third picks that are 150+ lbs, he's producing females that look better than most males. BGK's Debo is definitely on track to become a super-producer. Keep an eye on this boy as he heads towards becoming a legend just like his father.

BGK's Debo

Tri/Merle /Tri-Merle Influencers

The next four honorable mentions are XL American Bullies who have unique colors such as tris, tri-merles, and merles are changing the Bully game as we once knew it! The merle-color was originally perceived as a genetic flaw/ defect and all registries initially would not recognize them. Currently, merle/tri-merle American Bullies can only be registered with the ABKC. Tri-colored American Bullies can be registered with the UKC, ABKC, etc. In the beginning, most of the original American Bully breeders would stay away from merles and tri-merles, however, that has drastically changed now. The American Bully breed is constantly evolving. Due to their beautiful unique look, and "one of a kind" appeal, merles and tri-merles are rapidly becoming more dominant in the XL American Bully world. Tri-colored XL American Bullies used to be very rare, but that has also changed. There are still old-school breeders who refuse to deal with merles and tri-merles, but the general public have made it abundantly clear that they are willing to pay top dollar for a uniquely colored American Bully. The Bully market, much like any other, supply and demand dictate the marketplace. The following four impressive dogs changed the way XL American Bully breeders viewed this popular subgenre of Bullies. They carry all of the desired genotypes and phenotypes and rare character traits that the XL American Bully breeders love: blocky heads, wide chest, thick rears, sound temperaments, etc., and to make it even more appealing they topped it off with extremely unique 1 of a kind coats.

1. Bossy's Jumanji aka "JuJu"

Pedigree: https://www.pitpedia.com/dog/bossys-jumanji/

The first of these four is Bossy Kennel's Jumanji (aka Juju) who is a beautiful tri-merle dog, and even though he is a little short for the XL side, he is well put together. He has a thick rear, wide chest, girthy neck, and short back. Ultimately, he checks every box, not to mention he is stacked front to back, (almost resembling a chiseled bodybuilder)! Shoutout to Kat and Jumanji. Make sure to check out Bossy Kennels to see what else Jumanji has in store for the Bully community!

2. MBK's Morpheus

Pedigree: https://www.pitpedia.com/dog/morpheus/

The second on the list is another tri-merle which has changed the perception of tri-merles in the Bully world, MBK's Morpheus. He was produced by Dust Mundrick (who is a hidden gem among breeders as his blood keeps making an appearance, definitely one to look out for). Currently, he is owned by Ryan Guard of Monster Bully Kennels, who has been marketing him beautifully. This dog is a solid producer with a one-of-a-kind look. I'm not just saying that because I created and own his biggest son BGK's Gambino, I'm saying it because he is currently a crowd/Bully lover's favorite as his look is exotically intriguing. Everyone who sees him seems to fall in love with him. Currently, he's establishing a reputable name for himself among American Bully enthusiasts, and his pups go for top dollar because of his impressionable character traits and even temperament.

3. Scorpion Kennel's Woodland aka "Woodland"

Pedigree: https://www.pitpedia.com/dog/big-woodland-of-scorpion-kennels/

The third honorable mention is a personal favorite merle dog of mine, Scorpion Kennels, Woodland. If you want to talk about a merle Bully, there is no clearer depiction of a solid specimen than this dog. He is a beautiful lilac merle, and when you look at his size, his shoulders, his chest, his spread, his stance, his drive, his productions, he checks everything off of the list! If you didn't like merles before you saw him, he will **make** you reconsider after! Woodland is so impressive that it wouldn't matter what color he had, because in my eyes I would still find him awe-inspiring just off of his build alone. He's not impressive just because of his color, he's magnificent because of his genetic makeup, and the Bully attributes which he possesses. The fact that he is a lilac merle is an added bonus. Go check out Woodland of Scorpion Kennels!

4. Sunline's Omega

Pedigree: https://www.pitpedia.com/dog/sunlines-omega/

Sunline's Omega is one of the last on the tri/merles and tri-merles list, but please know that this by no means diminishes his contribution as an impactful tri-merle XL American Bully beast that he is. Omega is the total package, with or without his tri-merle suit. He has the thickness, the wide chest, and big blocky head as well as the signature Bully look, great topline, a strong rear, and a very solid temperament. He has proven himself to be an amazing producer with an incredible pedigree packed with XL producing power. In his pedigree, you will find BGK's Gaston, who is a son of BGK's The Rock, as well as some very solid blood from Probulls, so there is no question as to where he receives his top-quality production power from. This boy would be a top-quality American Bully in any color, so the fact that he is a tri-merle is icing on the cake. If he continues to be marketed and bred properly, he has the potential to be a future XL American Bully legend.

5. BGK's GAMBINO

Pedigree: https://www.pitpedia.com/dog/bgks-gambino/

Our last honorable mention, but definitely not least, is BGK's Gambino; the largest son of the infamous MBK's Morpheus. Most of the tri-merle XL American Bullies either have the structure or the incredible look/exotic coat, but not the true size that XL Bully is known for. BGK's Gambino is the youngest dog listed in this book for a damn good reason. Although he is young and currently in the process of proving himself as a super producer, BGK's Gambino is one of the *only* dogs on this list that has the rare combination of looks, structure, an exotic tri-merle coat, incredible XL size, as well as a perfect legend-filled pedigree.

MBK's Morpheus, BGK's Picasso, BGK's The Rock, UKC's Most Wanted Kimbo, XB's Icon, XB's Comet, etc. are all in this incredible Bully's beast of a pedigree. BGK's Gambino has started off with a bang as he is currently dropping some of the largest and best looking tri-merle puppies on the market with a very traditional XL American Bully genotype and phenotype that is highly sought after in today's XL American Bully community. This boy is rapidly growing in popularity and becoming a well-known superstar, and a highly sought-after stud! Here is one of BGKs's Gambino's first productions, BGK's King Crypto. This boy has an extremely unique and exotic look, and is a perfect example of the perfection BGK's Gambino is capable of producing!

BGK'S CRYPTO

Besides the fact that he is an incredibly impressive specimen of a tri-merle XL American Bully, BGK's Gambino has a faultless, loving, balanced temperament that all XL American Bully breeders are searching for. He is extremely loving and affectionate with my family members, and he also makes a strong guard dog when he is outside patrolling the yard. Gambino checks all of the boxes we have seen in the other legends mentioned, as well as the honorable mentions that are documented in this book. He shares the following characteristics with the previously discussed: stunning exotic looks, thick bone structure, huge head, wide chest, thick neck, great topline, impressive stance, and a bully-blocky body. Please keep an eye on this emerging legend as he makes a huge impact on the evolution of the XL American Bully scene.

128

BIG GEMINI KENNELS
BGK'S GAMBINO

I hope that you have enjoyed this journey as much as I have, and have learned something along the way regarding which dogs helped to shape and influence the XL American Bully breed into what it is today. This young breed is still evolving and morphing into something new and exciting. If you look through both the legends and the honorable mentions lists, you will notice some similar traits are preferred by the Bully community, and I don't see it changing in the foreseeable future. We like to see things overdone while still upholding the Bully standard for the most part. Physical traits such as big blocky heads, a sinister look, large dogs with impeccable structure, great muscle tone, solid temperaments, and a certain "wow" factor that is hard to articulate are the most sought-out. The "wow" factor is hard to explain through words alone, and that is why I found it to be necessary to include pictures and video links for you to be able to see them for yourself in order to fully comprehend why the XL American Bully is such an astounding companion dog. The breed is moving forward to creating an even larger impact on the dog world. Currently, more and more breeders are health testing their stock, to make sure future generations are healthy as possible and do not just simply carry the size and look of their ancestors. This is the way to make sure you improve the breed. Due to their beautiful unique look, and "one of one" appeal, tris, merles, and tri-merles are becoming increasingly more dominant in the XL American Bully world. There are still old school breeders who refuse to deal with merles and tri-merles, but the general public has made it clear that they are willing to pay top dollar for uniquely colored American Bullies, and like any other market, supply and demand dictates the success of the marketplace. Be sure to look for the names that you have seen in this book in the pedigree of any dog you are looking to purchase or breed because they will most certainly add a tremendous amount of credit and quality to your dog or breeding program. As I have previously stated, I am a top-quality breeder, an animal lover, a dog connoisseur, and a true American Bully enthusiast at heart who has been around since the beginning. Many members of the American Bully community have labeled me an "OG", however, what I truly am is a dog historian. My goal with this book is to preserve and document this moment in Bully history for generations to come in order for people to learn more about where the XL American Bully started and what it has now become, as well as the legendary dogs which helped to solidify it. My wish is that you will take the information that I have given you here in this book and create, (or buy), dogs that are even more special and more noteworthy than past breeders have done, using this information as one of the tools to do so. Knowledge is power. Arm yourself, my friend. These dogs are tried and true, heavily desired, and incredibly impressive. These are the XL American Bully Legends. God Bless.

Yours Truly,

Andre Smith

Big Gemini Kennels, Quality Matters!

www.BigGeminiKennels.com

www.instagram.com/largestpitbulls

A special thank you goes out to my daughter and writing partner Racquel Smith for assisting me in writing this book. Currently, she is in the process of writing her own murder mystery novel entitled "Dead to Me" which will be coming out soon! Please support and don't miss out! - *Andre Smith*

*"I would like to extend a big thank you to my co-author and daughter, Racquel. She has been around the breed since the day she was born, and is incredibly intelligent, articulate, as well as a brilliant writer. BGK's The Rock was also her best friend and housemate as well. I couldn't have asked for better help. I am glad we were able to create this piece of XL American Bully history together. I love you."- **Andre Smith**

Acknowledgements
(Dead to Me)

By Racquel Smith

(Book coming soon): After the mysterious death of their friend, a group of unknowing graduates are in for an unusual college experience. When Casey Johnson gets accepted into her dream college, she quickly learns that it won't be easy to fit in without her best friend by her side. Her old friend group had disbanded shortly after Kennedy Perrish's death. **But what happens when you start to see your dead best friend around campus?**

RIP TO ALL THE AMAZING XL AMERICAN BULLIES THAT HELPED SHAPE THIS EVOLVING BREED.

Printed in Great Britain
by Amazon

43272437R00082